This book has b
with the Christ
Society has existed since 1870 to present the fundamental truths of Christianity to enquirers. Its address is:

1 Little Cloister
Westminster Abbey
London
SW1P 3PL

Other titles in this series:

Why God?
Why Pray?
Why Belief?
Why Suffering?
Finding God in Later Life
Finding God in Bereavement
Finding God in Illness

Finding God in Marriage Breakdown

Simon Ridley

LION PUBLISHING

Copyright © 1997 Simon Ridley
The author asserts the moral right to be identified as the author of this work

This edition published in 1997 by Lion Publishing plc
Sandy Lane West, Oxford, England
ISBN 0 7459 3719 5

Albatross Books Pty Ltd PO Box 320, Sutherland, NSW 2232, Australia I
ISBN 0 7324 1594 2

First edition 1997
10 9 8 7 6 5 4 3 2 1 0

All rights reserved
A catalogue record for this book is
available from the British Library
Printed and bound in India by Ajanta

*For Mary and Ginny
with love*

Finding God in Marriage Breakdown

'Archbishop demands health warning for divorce.' Under this headline *The Times* of Tuesday 29 August, 1995, reported that the Roman Catholic Archbishop of Cashel and Emly, addressing weekend pilgrims in County Tipperary, had told them that 'divorced people smoked and drank more than their married counterparts. They were also liable to experience eating and sleeping problems as well as stress, anger, pain, a deep sense of loss, and a lack of self esteem.'

My first reaction was fairly dismissive. 'Well, he would say that, wouldn't he?' Ireland was heading towards a referendum on the ban on divorce, which forms part of that country's written constitution. A similar poll nine years earlier had resulted in a two to one majority in favour of retaining the ban, but the pressure for change had been unrelenting, and the church was fearful of the outcome this time. They were right to be. By the narrowest of majorities it went against them.

My second response was much closer to home than Tipperary. I experienced that very uncomfortable feeling a good preacher can cause you, when he seems to cast not only his words but also his beady eye suddenly in your direction. 'How on earth does this man know all this about *me?*'

It is true. I smoke like Thomas the Tank, and I have to watch it with the gin bottle. I live daily with a wretched condition known politely as IBS, and insomnia is a not infrequent night visitor. As for the rest—stress, anger, pain, a deep sense of loss and lack of self-esteem—I know them all well enough. And I can trace most of this back to the break-up of my first marriage more than twenty years ago.

Suffering

As far as I am concerned, therefore, it does appear that the good Archbishop is probably right, and I am sure I am not alone. As always there will be exceptions, and you do hear of couples, especially in show business, who seem to be able to change partners with rather less anguish than moving house. Curiously, however, this is only very rarely the case with people one actually knows. One must wonder if it is all quite so simple and straightforward as William Hickey or Nigel Dempster would have us believe, or indeed so sleazy as we often like to imagine from the stuff that sells newspapers from lower down Grub Street. It is easy to forget that all these stories are about real men and women, no doubt with bodies more beautiful but with a heart, mind, spirit, not unlike our own. There, behind the glamorous pictures and the salacious gossip, is probably misery.

It so happens that I started writing this on holiday in France. My morning chore was to walk down into our little town to buy the baguette and get *Le Var Nice-Matin* so that we might try to fathom the weather forecast over breakfast. It is rather a good paper, but almost as local as the baguette. The editor has clearly decided that only very few items of world news will be of any interest whatever to his readers, but nearly every day he gave them yet more gossip about our hapless Royals, and one morning almost the only thing that had happened around the globe was this: Elizabeth Taylor had been taken to hospital with heart problems. Now there, you would have thought, was a tough cookie, she of the two Oscars and seven marriages. But is she? As *Le Var* pointed out, this illness came just after she had instigated separation proceedings, yet again, after four years of her latest marriage, and we were reminded that the poor lady had been in hospital for three months in 1990, which was last time round, suffering from 'graves problèmes respiratoires'—it sounds far worse in French! Maybe even the stars are not immune.

Certainly, for the great majority of lesser mortals separation and divorce mean suffering. Suffering all round. The report in *The Times* I have referred to goes on to suggest that the Irish Archbishop has a weight of research on his side with statistical evidence from a wide range of reputable organizations, and clear indications from across Europe and the United States of the link between marital breakdown and physical and mental ill health, and according to the World Health Organization, suicide. Small wonder the Archbishop suggests that 'divorce should carry a Government health warning'.

Where is God?

But I hope that is not all he had to say on the subject to the pilgrims in Tipperary. Did he also speak to them about the will and the ways of God when things go wrong? Can one experience God at all in the breakdown of a marriage (and indeed in the breakdown of other totally committed relationships)? Can one find him in the agonies of separation and divorce, not to mention the trials and tribulations so often lying in wait in a second or subsequent marriage? I expect he did, but such words, even from an Archbishop, do not sell newspapers, so they were not fully reported. And did he go on to tell them how his church and the churches generally should address these very real problems? What they might do to help pick up the pieces? I rather fear he may not have done so. His audience would have known his answer all too well. It would be like asking Margaret Thatcher whether we should open the floodgates to Europe: No, No, No. But will that do? Has the Christian church really no more to offer than a repeated negative? It is the object of this short booklet to probe these questions and to see if one can offer a tentative hint or two at some possible answers.

But how can I possibly hope to do so when the circumstances of my marriage breakdown were probably so very different from a particular situation which perhaps concerns you now? I know nothing at first hand about the agonies of being deserted by someone you love and have cared for, the father/mother of the children you share and both adore, when he/she goes off with another who, for good measure, may very well have been a friend. I cannot tell you what it is like, or what I would do, when one's solemn marriage vow 'for better for worse, for richer for poorer, in sickness and in health' is taxed beyond the limits of endurance by a partner's flagrant and repeated infidelities, or by verbal and physical violence, or abuse of your children, or addiction to drink or drugs or, not infrequently, to a job, or gambling away all that you both possess—not to mention the unbearable strains which may be placed upon a marriage by redundancy or financial collapse.

Still less can I imagine some completely unforeseen change in the one you marry: manic depression to the point of schizophrenia, for example, or the discovery of practising homosexuality. I can imagine the distress, but I cannot tell you how I would cope with it, if I had entered into a marriage longing for children and found that my partner was unable or, far worse, simply unwilling to have them. And I can only say the same of the horrors of a marriage which rapidly turns out, for one or for both, to be a sexual catastrophe, a dreaded nightmare, even from night one.

I have no real experience of the marriage which gradually but remorselessly falls apart, through no obvious fault, but simply because one partner grows deeply away from the other so that you both just know, especially when the children have flown, that you simply have nothing at all in common any more. I cannot speak with any authority of the terrible ennui of many marriages when all the early passion is spent, and instead of developing naturally and comfortably into loving companionship you are left only with King Lear's 'dull, stale, tired bed', and worse still, staring silently at each other in a total collapse of all communication.

What is missing from this catalogue of woes? It does not pretend to be exhaustive, because the sad truth is that the capacity of the human race to make a mess of marriage is almost limitless. It may be that you have picked up this little book because you are yourself in the midst of separation and divorce or still suffering as a result of it all, or because you have a deep concern for some person or a couple—perhaps one of your children's marriages—in the throes of this experience. If so, you may find that I have still not touched upon the actual situation which affects you.

Certainly there is one glaring omission from the catalogue above. It does not mention the man who, believing profoundly in God—albeit in rather conventional fashion—and sincerely believing himself to be happily married, suddenly after fourteen years (the seven year itch x 2?) goes completely off the rails, and at the dangerous age of thirty-nine (the male menopause?) falls hopelessly for another man's wife. She is thirty-nine also, so the dangers are compounded. In no time at all the situation is out of control. Driven as if by the Furies in a Greek tragedy, he struggles—indeed they both do, desperately—but the die is cast. After apparently endless and destructive prevarication he separates from his deeply wounded and still loving wife; he is eventually divorced for his adultery and he marries the lady in question, her first marriage also having ended in many tears.

It so happens that I am that man. I happen also to be a priest in the Church of England, and if that is not enough, the other partner in the marriage I broke up, was and is a deeply committed and devout Roman Catholic. It was bad; so bad that at first I declined vigorously to attempt the task of writing this because even now, having recently celebrated the twentieth anniversary of that second wedding, it is almost unbearably painful to relive the events that led up to it, or to recall the suffering I caused to those I loved, not to mention the utter misery, to the point nearly of self-destruction, which I brought upon myself.

I was, however, persuaded to try to put pen to paper (happily, on holiday in France—one still has to do these things in the old-fashioned way!) because, going through that fire, I learned much. I also had to unlearn much. And if any of that can be of any help to anyone, then so be it.

But the experience of marriage breakdown is intensely personal. Two factors which particularly mark my own were: first, that it was the ending of a *happy marriage*, and second, that I happen to be a clergyman. It is unlikely, if my earlier catalogue had not already covered a personal situation of yours, that this personal addendum will now have done so, although it has to be said that the breakdown of an apparently happy marriage is far more common than one might suppose, and hence perhaps so much of the grief and the guilt. And, alas, it is also a fact that clergy and their wives (and soon, no doubt, their husbands) feature increasingly in the ever-rising tally of divorces each year in a way that was virtually unknown until quite recently.

But that is not the point. I am not here trying to speak directly to any particular situation. I am not even a trained marriage guidance counsellor, although in my fifteen years as a parson, in various parishes at home and abroad, I had my fair share of trying to help. I did not know then, and I do not know now, what the answer may be for any particular tormented couple facing these difficulties. But I hope and believe that I may know a man who does. I am speaking, I hope not irreverently, of God, sharing our lot completely in Jesus, and working so strongly, but sometimes very strangely, through his Spirit. If God is God then there is nothing, but nothing, outside his ken. And there is nowhere, but nowhere, he cannot help.

Nowhere? Are we quite certain of that? There are some areas of life where we are inclined to assume God's writ does not run. Certainly for people of my generation, growing up to adulthood in the fifties—that is to say shortly before the Flood—sex was one of them. Sex was out-of-bounds for God. All that He seemed to have to say on the subject was the seventh and the easiest to remember (if not to keep) of the Ten Commandments. For many of us who were still virgins, incredibly by today's standards, right up to marriage and well into our twenties, 'thou shalt not commit adultery' was still a rather distant hurdle. There was much ground to be covered first! To be honest, the fact that sex was assumed to be none of God's business rather added to the piquancy of our first fumbling adventures into love. Only, however, until things went wrong. I had my first experience of this as a young undergraduate at Oxford. I cannot forbear to mention that my tutor there, at Magdalen, was the great C S Lewis. Looking for all the world like a bluff farmer he was in fact nothing of the kind, and I find it bizarre (and so to be fair, would he) that there should recently have been some talk of making him a saint! Seemingly a cold fish, he was in fact a dark horse. Recognized as the great expert on courtly love of a bygone age, it came as no great surprise to me when he was himself 'surprised by joy', and entered upon that romance of marriage and shared suffering which half the world now knows as *Shadowlands*. Perhaps a modicum of this rubbed off on me. I fell, desperately, for the most beautiful girl in the world. For many of us in the early 1950s—and not just the sheltered sons of the manse—these things were all the more intense just because they were unconsummated (though sometimes it was a wonderfully close-run thing). We were innocents then. It was an idyll which could not last, but love is blind, they say, and when my love wrote and told me just before her eighteenth birthday, that she was going to marry a man nearly twice her age, I thought I would die. I did not die, of course, but life would never be quite the same.

A few months earlier my father, whom I adored, had died after a short and terrible illness. I was twenty. This double bereavement, for that is precisely what the end of a deeply loving relationship can be, came as a first frightening experience of God hiding himself. It was to be many years before I was to understand that God is as much to be found in sex as in everything else, and sometimes supremely so. He is after all the creator of all things, and it is perverse in the extreme to imagine that he is not to be found in sex when we all know, somewhat obsessively nowadays, that this is what makes his world go round.

If this was how I felt about sex and God, and how I suspect many still feel, even in our recently discovered Brave Free World, the reasons are plain enough, and I am afraid the church has a lot to answer for, starting perhaps as long ago as St Paul himself. We inherit 2,000 years of Flesh and the things of

Man set starkly against Spirit and the things of God: and of course sex is Flesh, or so the story goes. I have come to believe that this exaggerated dichotomy is profoundly damaging and impossible to reconcile with the central fact of our Christian faith: God made Man, not just vaguely and generally Man, but an attractive full-blooded man, tempted in all points like we are.

It results in a church which, once it has lost the power to boss people about, finds itself marooned from vast areas of basic human experience, often the very areas where men and women would otherwise be most likely to find God and sometimes, as in the case of separation and divorce, where they most desperately need him. And the tragedy is this: after so many centuries of such distortion, an increasingly secular world not only expects to find this sort of church, but has almost come to prefer it that way. And so it is that ordinary folk cannot believe that their local church in town or village can really be for the likes of them, and more especially if they are in a right old mess, as most of us quite often are.

And the clergy? Well, if they are Roman Catholic they have to be celibate: no sex, you know. All a bit odd, and not surprising that some of them do find it a bit difficult, and seem to get round it one way or another, but of course he can't marry. After all, he is the priest, isn't he? And if they are C of E or Methodist, or whatever, oh well, they can marry of course—probably best if they do! But we don't expect the Reverend and his wife to carry on like the rest of us.

One has to say that some clergy do seem almost to ask for this nonsense, but many absolutely hate it, just as they hate the 'beg your pardon, Vicar', which so often accompanies the blue joke or the rich language. All this is decidedly unhealthy, and betokens a church out of touch with humanity.

In an extreme case a local church can soon be seen only as a place of refuge for a handful of the very elderly and the occasional crank, presided over by a cardboard minister whom everyone assumes, rightly or wrongly, to have little or no knowledge of real life. It can become a total travesty of Christianity and light years away from the Jesus of the Gospels.

Does Jesus *really* share in our suffering?

Let us be ruthlessly honest. Even with Jesus himself, is there not a difficulty? A full-blooded real man, tempted like us? Is that really true? The Epistle to the Hebrews does not stop there: 'Tempted in all points like as we are: and yet without spot of sin.'

Having been reasonably well schooled I am not unaware of the central importance of those additional words in Christian theology. Without them one learns that the whole doctrine of redemption might be blown apart. But how I have sometimes yearned for it to be otherwise. Sometimes one is sorely tempted to say 'hang theology'! We may be able to survive cardboard clergymen, but a cardboard Christ would be unbearable. Did he really go through the mill as we have to? Of course he suffered, and the cross has been a beacon of hope to countless millions, but does his Passion touch upon our human passions? How does he truly share our temptations, our failures and yes, our sins?

The only honest answer I can give is that I am not sure, and I am bound to say that for our troubled times it would have been helpful, to say the least, to know a little more of Christ's sexuality. Clearly he is good and loving and kind, and he reaches out to touch so much in our human condition. He can be very strong and even fierce in indignation. He tells us, shows us, so much about God. But did he fall in love? Did he fall out of love? And if so how did he handle these emotional upheavals? The Gospels are remarkably silent.

After all the stained glass windows, it comes as something of a relief to find that there are some very real people among the closest followers of Jesus. That, surely, is why Peter is such a favourite, and Doubting Thomas. Even Judas strikes a frightening chord in us. And thank heavens for Mary Magdalen! But what about Jesus himself? What were his feelings for her, for example, or perhaps, as some have suggested darkly, for John, 'the beloved disciple'? We simply do not know. And what he has to say directly on sexual matters generally is pretty sparse and sometimes enigmatic, though at least we can all cling to the resounding words when the unhappy woman was taken in adultery: 'Let him that is among you without sin cast the first stone.'

You may recall how Nikos Kazantzakis

treated that incident in his novel *Zorba the Greek*. Both the book, and the marvellous film they made of it, were major milestones in my Christian journey when they first came out. In his other great book, *The Last Temptation*, which got him into serious trouble with the Vatican, and which Martin Scorsese's film made even more notorious, Jesus and Mary Magdalen make passionate love under a flowing lemon tree, and afterwards Jesus says to her, 'I never knew the world was so beautiful or the flesh so holy. It too is a daughter of God, a graceful sister of the soul... I never knew the joys of the body were not sinful.' Can this be right? No: it turns out to be only a dream in his dying moments on the cross.

The Last Temptation is an unforgettable book, which the author himself describes as 'the confession of every man who struggles', and for those who do see things as he does in terms of 'the incessant, merciless battle fought between the spirit and the flesh' it could open the window upon God. But not for me. For me, Zorba was the one. The story of this zany man (played magnificently by Anthony Quinn) attaching himself to the bookish stranger and turning his life upside down, by bringing everything miraculously alive, made Christ more real for me than a thousand sermons.

One evening, sitting alone in a very cold flat in London at a very bad moment all those years ago, I spotted that the film was coming on late on the telly. I decided to stay up and see it again. As I say, the first time had been a milestone: this time was a turning point. I was not alone after all. God was in on the whole ghastly business. The mysterious gaps in the Gospels no longer mattered. There was no doubt any more that Jesus had been here before me. He did know and he would help. God, who had been hiding himself, had returned, *down his own secret stair*. And I prayed, as I had never prayed before.

God helped me

I will not pretend that it was all plain sailing after that, but having once turned that one big corner I began to see more hopeful signs all over the place, and looking back now I do not doubt that God was at work. Within days I happened to bump into an old friend in the street - someone I had not seen for ages - and he invited me to join him and his wife and friends for a weekend at their cottage in Dorset. Having become a recluse I had to summon the courage to go, but it was meant to be, and I came back to my dreary job in the Civil Service lighter of step. I had been taken out of myself and the appalling slough of self-pity. I came to appreciate more the simple kindness of colleagues at work—my Roman Catholic boss, the spinster lady with whom I shared an office, the jolly girl who made the tea. Until then every working day had been a Black Monday, and sometimes I hardly knew how I would get there. But I came to value the discipline and even the drudgery (because I can assure you that scrutinizing Housing Compulsory Purchase Orders is hardly a ton of fun). Morning and evening I began to make myself walk to the station across St James's Park and I started once more to notice the sheer beauty of nature, even in the heart of London. In the evening I became more content to sit quietly in my little flat rather than go prowling around looking for tawdry excitement without the courage to indulge it.

There was also a small group of people, each and every one of whom I shall always remember with gratitude and affection for the help they gave in many different ways throughout that time. Chief among them was a clever old psychiatrist, to whom someone had steered me, thinking, probably quite rightly, that I had gone a bit mad. He said very little, but he missed nothing, and it is probably not too much to say that he may have saved my life, because I was ready to do anything to escape from my self-inflicted misery and indecision. I believe that like so many in his profession he was an Austrian Jew, and I have no doubt whatsoever that God was very present in his patient, healing work.

There were others too. One of the many problems in the break-up of a marriage is that it can cause havoc among immediate family and friends. Loyalties are divided; long-standing relationships are placed under severe strain; rival camps are formed. One becomes aware, having had a surfeit of advice (none of which is taken) that one is an embarrassment or, even worse, a bore. The result is that one tends to hide away, or to look to others for some sort of companionship. There were the men, and then there were also the girls. But it would not be appropriate here to do more than say a heartfelt thank you to them. Among the men was one in particular. He was an old bachelor friend, but I had rather lost touch with him. When the time came he took me in and after six weeks or so he pushed me out and helped me to get established on my own, but thereafter at regular intervals the summons came to supper—he was an excellent cook—and incidentally a homosexual and a devout high Anglican. Sometimes he would drag me off to evening mass at All Saints, Margaret Street or the Ascension, Marble Arch (higher still), and then we would spend a long evening chain-smoking, drinking his devilish dry Martinis and good wine, and talking about everything under the sun *except my problems*. He is dead now. All I can say is may God bless him!

God was undoubtedly at work also in the

sheer down-to-earth goodness and old-fashioned civilized Christian conduct of my abandoned wife. She was cruelly hurt, but stoic and Scottish she got on with her life, making it a priority to give a simple but stable home to our two young daughters, never letting them doubt that we both loved them, always making it easy for me to see them. She put up with endless tearful self-indulgent telephone calls from me and repeated attempts at reconciliation. And when all this finally failed, and we agreed that she should divorce me, there was none of the all-too-common and bitter warring about money or possessions or anything else, all of which is usually of no benefit to anybody except highly-paid divorce lawyers, and which, above all, can do untold harm to the children. What we never for one moment forgot is that we had indeed loved one another; that we had happily shared much over many years; that we were and would always be the joint parents of our children, to whom we both had a most solemn responsibility; and that hopefully we should not cease to be friends. That is how it has turned out, and I thank God for it, and I believe our now grown-up and married daughters thank God for it too. Others of course may well not be so fortunate, but if there is one simple message from my experience it would be this: If a marriage must end then for heaven's sake, as far as humanly possible, let it be without enduring acrimony. That *must* be what God would want.

If a marriage must end... That is the question. Things will go wrong. They always have and alas they always will. After all, we are told that marriages are not made in heaven and that is all too obvious sometimes. People change, and we have seen that there is a whole raft of other reasons why a marriage may break down, gradually or suddenly. So, separation and divorce there will be. Divorce, which in this country until a hundred years ago was almost impossible, except for the very rich and powerful, has now probably become too easy, and there is rapidly increasing alarm about the social and economic cost. The Joseph Rowntree Foundation has recently shown what common sense has always told us, that the children of broken homes can suffer terribly as a result of their parents' divorce, and frequently end up in trouble of one kind or another. Whatever new legislation there may or may not be, couples—whether legally married or not—have got to recover the sense of awesome responsibility of bringing a child into the world, and must, wherever possible, learn again to put this before their own purely selfish desire for happiness.

This must sound strange and pretty rich coming from one who appears to have failed in exactly this regard, but neither my wife nor I are in any way proud of what we did. We hope and pray for forgiveness, from God and from those we hurt. We pray too, against all the statistical odds, that none of our five children will have to go through this traumatic ordeal. We have now had many good years together—stormy sometimes; let no one think that a second marriage will be a bed of roses!—but we accept that life will always be something of a compromise, second best. Certainly, for those who call themselves Christians, and indeed for those who simply aspire to be responsible citizens, divorce is not something to be 'enterprised, nor taken in hand, unadvisedly, lightly or wantonly,' any more than marriage itself. Nevertheless, for some it will happen, even for some devout Christians, not excluding faithful clergymen, and even the odd bishop or two. Why? Simply because we are all human, and because we live in the world as it unfortunately is.

The position of the Church

Where does this leave the churches? To be frank, in a ghastly muddle. Quite rightly, in my view, they still stand firmly for the ideal of a life-long union of one man and one woman in Christian marriage, but they cannot ignore the world around them. So they try to make some sort of accommodation with it. Some of the Reformed Churches, notably in this country the Presbyterians, have always been prepared to perform a second marriage in church, and some are even flirting with divorce ceremonies. The Roman Catholics resort to what some find often to be the dishonest device of nullity, the authorities satisfying themselves that for one reason or another the first marriage—despite three or four strapping children perhaps—was not a marriage at all, so everyone is free to start all over again.

The Church of England is probably even more dishonest. The official line is quite simple: no re-marriage in church for divorced persons, who should be directed to the Registry Office, where conveniently a civil ceremony can always be arranged. Nevertheless, out of pastoral considerations, a second marriage may in certain circumstances be 'blessed' in church. Certainly that is how the official 'service of prayer and dedication' is widely understood. Until quite recently this was a quiet and private affair, but latterly it has become virtually indistinguishable from a first wedding, with all the frills, and with the ultimate public approval of society-people appearing in *Hello!* magazine, complete with smiling bishop in full purple. I believe there is a widespread feeling that this just won't do, and the C of E should make up its mind one way or the other.

We may in fact not have very far to look

for the answer. I have long thought that the Eastern Orthodox Churches have got it right. They do not, of course, pretend that divorce and remarriage are a good thing, but they have adopted a pragmatic approach which ordinary folk both understand and respect. A second marriage is permitted, following a divorce, but it rightly contains a penitential element. Even a third marriage is possible but the ceremony is short and sharp, including a remarkable prayer referring to Rahab the Harlot, and quoting St Paul's 'it is better to marry than to burn'. And that, reasonably enough, is your lot. A Byzantine Emperor, rejoicing in the name of Leo the Philosopher, caused a serious schism by his fourth marriage! It seems to me that the Orthodox practice combines due discipline with honest realism, and necessary pastoral care with essential penitence, and the rest of the Christian world would do well to study it carefully.

But it is certainly not for me to start telling the churches what they should or should not do. Nor was that in any way a principal object of this little book. Its purpose has been simply to show how one man came through the experience and the suffering at the ending of a marriage, losing God and being found again by him. That is all, but it is everything. May he find you too—*down his own secret stair*, as the Scottish poet George MacDonald so memorably put it:

> O son of man, to right my lot
> Nought but thy presence can avail;
> Yet on the road thy wheels are not,
>   Nor on the sea thy sail!

My fancied ways why should'st
thou heed?
Thou com'st down thine own
secret stair;
Com'st down to answer all my need,
Yea, every bygone prayer!

GEORGE MACDONALD